YOU GOT THIS

summersdale

YOU GOT THIS

An Hachette UK Company
www.hachette.co.uk

Summersdale Publishers Ltd
Part of Octopus Publishing Group Limited
Carmelite House
50 Victoria Embankment
LONDON
EC4Y 0DZ
UK

www.summersdale.com

Printed and bound in the Czech Republic

ISBN: 978-1-78685-040-9

Substantial discounts on bulk quantities of Summersdale books are available to corporations, professional associations and other organisations. For details contact general enquiries: telephone: +44 (0) 1243 771107 or email: enquiries@summersdale.com.

TO ....Alice....

FROM ....Lori....

♡♡   OOPS!   ♡♡

Dear Darling Lori

You don't need any advice because you know exactly what you are doing!!!

TRUST THYSELF:
EVERY HEART VIBRATES
TO THAT IRON STRING.

Ralph Waldo Emerson

But here is a little book of wisdom to show my love for you!

xx ♡ ♡ ♡ ♡ ♡ ♡ ♡♡ xx

NO ONE CAN MAKE YOU FEEL INFERIOR WITHOUT YOUR CONSENT.

Eleanor Roosevelt

WE HAVE TO DARE
TO BE OURSELVES,
HOWEVER
FRIGHTENING
OR STRANGE
THAT SELF MIGHT
PROVE TO BE.

May Sarton

I AM THE MASTER OF
MY FATE: I AM THE
CAPTAIN OF MY SOUL.

William Ernest Henley

YOU CAN ACHIEVE WHATEVER YOU WANT TO.

DO WHAT YOU CAN,
WITH WHAT YOU HAVE,
WHERE YOU ARE.

Theodore Roosevelt

ORIGINALITY
IMPLIES BEING
BOLD ENOUGH TO
GO BEYOND
ACCEPTED NORMS.

Anthony Storr

BELIEVE IN YOURSELF AND THE REST WILL HAPPEN.

WHO SEEKS
SHALL FIND.

Sophocles

WE ARE SHAPED
BY OUR THOUGHTS.
WE BECOME WHAT
WE THINK.

Buddha

IT IS NOT POSSIBLE TO
GO FORWARD WHILE
LOOKING BACK.

Ludwig Mies van der Rohe

BELIEVE IN LIFE! ALWAYS
HUMAN BEINGS WILL
LIVE AND PROGRESS TO
GREATER, BROADER
AND FULLER LIFE.

W. E. B. Du Bois

JUST BE
YOURSELF. THERE
IS NO ONE BETTER.

Taylor Swift

THERE IS JUST
ONE LIFE FOR
EACH OF US:
OUR OWN.

Euripides

TRUST YOURSELF.
YOU KNOW MORE
THAN YOU THINK
YOU DO.

Benjamin Spock

GIVE IT YOUR ALL.

I AM NOT
A HAS-BEEN.
I AM A WILL BE.

Lauren Bacall

EVERYONE'S DREAM CAN COME TRUE IF YOU JUST STICK TO IT AND WORK HARD.

Serena Williams

DON'T SPEND TOO MUCH TIME THINKING — JUST DO.

IF YOU'RE
PRESENTING YOURSELF
WITH CONFIDENCE, YOU
CAN PULL OFF PRETTY
MUCH ANYTHING.

Katy Perry

TELL ME, WHAT IS
IT YOU PLAN TO
DO WITH YOUR
ONE WILD AND
PRECIOUS LIFE?

Mary Oliver

BEGIN TO BE NOW
WHAT YOU WILL
BE HEREAFTER.

William James

MIGHTY OAKS
FROM LITTLE
ACORNS GROW.

Anonymous

BE YOURSELF. THE
WORLD WORSHIPS
THE ORIGINAL.

Ingrid Bergman

BELIEVE IN YOUR CAPABILITIES.

LIFE IS LIKE RIDING
A BICYCLE. TO KEEP
YOUR BALANCE, YOU
MUST KEEP MOVING.

Albert Einstein

WITH CONFIDENCE,
YOU HAVE WON
EVEN BEFORE YOU
HAVE STARTED.

Marcus Garvey

ALWAYS ACT LIKE YOU'RE WEARING AN INVISIBLE CROWN.

Anonymous

AS SOON AS YOU
TRUST YOURSELF,
YOU WILL KNOW
HOW TO LIVE.

Johann Wolfgang von Goethe

YOU'RE STRONGER THAN
YOU BELIEVE. DON'T LET
YOUR FEAR OWN YOU.
OWN YOURSELF.

Michelle Hodkin

YOU CAN'T TRUST
OTHER PEOPLE. IF IT'S
IMPORTANT, YOU HAVE
TO DO IT YOURSELF.

Neil Gaiman

YOU CAN'T BE STOPPED.

WE FALL
FORWARD
TO SUCCEED.

Mary Kay Ash

IF YOU WORK REALLY
HARD, AND YOU'RE
KIND, AMAZING
THINGS WILL HAPPEN.

Conan O'Brien

BE WHO YOU ARE
AND SAY WHAT YOU FEEL,
BECAUSE THOSE WHO
MIND DON'T MATTER,
AND THOSE WHO
MATTER DON'T MIND.

Bernard Baruch

GO CONFIDENTLY
IN THE DIRECTION
OF YOUR DREAMS!
LIVE THE LIFE
YOU'VE IMAGINED.

Henry David Thoreau

YOU ARE GOOD,
YOU ARE GREAT,
YOU ARE AMAZING.

Austin Carlile

I DO NOT BELIEVE IN TAKING RIGHT DECISIONS. I TAKE A DECISION AND MAKE IT RIGHT.

Muhammad Ali Jinnah

IF YOU BELIEVE IN YOURSELF EVERYONE ELSE WILL TOO.

LIVE BOLDLY.
PUSH YOURSELF.
DON'T SETTLE.

Jojo Moyes

ACCEPT THE CHALLENGES
SO THAT YOU CAN FEEL
THE EXHILARATION
OF VICTORY.

George S. Patton

IF YOU THINK
YOU CAN DO IT,
YOU CAN.

John Burroughs

YOU HAVE THE
ANSWER. JUST GET
QUIET ENOUGH TO
HEAR IT.

Pat Obuchowski

TRUST YOUR INSTINCTS; YOU KNOW WHAT TO DO.

EVERY MAN IS THE
ARCHITECT OF HIS
OWN FORTUNE.

Appius Claudius Caecus

A STRONG, POSITIVE
SELF-IMAGE IS THE BEST
POSSIBLE PREPARATION
FOR SUCCESS.

Joyce Brothers

NO ONE
ELSE CAN
DO WHAT
YOU CAN.

DIG WITHIN. THERE
LIES THE WELL-
SPRING OF GOOD:
EVER DIG AND IT
WILL EVER FLOW.

Marcus Aurelius

EVEN IF YOU FALL ON
YOUR FACE, YOU'RE STILL
MOVING FORWARD.

Victor Kiam

YOU ARE WHAT
YOU BELIEVE
YOURSELF TO BE.

Paulo Coelho

DON'T GIVE UP.
DON'T LOSE HOPE.
DON'T SELL OUT.

Christopher Reeve

THERE
IS ONLY
ONE YOU,
SO BE
YOU!

ACCEPT WHO
YOU ARE; AND
REVEL IN IT.

Mitch Albom

STEP BY STEP
AND THE THING
IS DONE.

Charles Atlas

NO ONE KNOWS
WHAT HE CAN DO
UNTIL HE TRIES.

Publilius Syrus

TRUST IN YOURSELF.

THROW CAUTION
TO THE WIND AND
JUST DO IT.

Carrie Underwood

LIFE ISN'T ABOUT FINDING
YOURSELF. LIFE IS ABOUT
CREATING YOURSELF.

George Bernard Shaw

RISE TO THE CHALLENGE.

FORTUNE
FAVOURS
THE BOLD.

Latin proverb

IF YOU CANNOT DO GREAT THINGS, DO SMALL THINGS IN A GREAT WAY.

Napoleon Hill

WHATEVER YOU CAN DO
OR DREAM YOU CAN,
BEGIN IT; BOLDNESS HAS
GENIUS, POWER AND
MAGIC IN IT.

Johann Wolfgang von Goethe

PROVE YOURSELF WRONG.

YOU HAVE
TO BELIEVE IN
YOURSELF.

Sun Tzu

DO YOU WANT TO
KNOW WHO YOU ARE?
DON'T ASK. ACT! ACTION
WILL DELINEATE AND
DEFINE YOU.

Witold Gombrowicz

TO ACCOMPLISH
GREAT THINGS WE
MUST NOT ONLY ACT,
BUT ALSO DREAM;
NOT ONLY PLAN,
BUT ALSO BELIEVE.

Anatole France

LIVE AS IF YOU WERE
TO DIE TOMORROW.
LEARN AS IF YOU WERE
TO LIVE FOREVER.

Mahatma Gandhi

LEAVE YOUR EXCUSES AND LIVE YOUR DREAMS!

Paul F. Davis

BELIEVE IN YOURSELF
AND YOU CAN ACHIEVE
GREATNESS IN YOUR LIFE.

Judy Blume

COURAGE WILL TAKE YOU TO ALL SORTS OF PLACES.

I CARE NOT SO
MUCH WHAT I AM
TO OTHERS AS WHAT
I AM TO MYSELF.

Michel de Montaigne

DOUBT KILLS
MORE DREAMS
THAN FAILURE
EVER WILL.

Suzy Kassem

THE MAN WHO
REMOVES A MOUNTAIN
BEGINS BY CARRYING
AWAY SMALL STONES.

Confucius

TO BELIEVE
YOURSELF BRAVE
IS TO BE BRAVE; IT
IS THE ONE ONLY
ESSENTIAL THING.

Mark Twain

NO GREAT
DISCOVERY WAS
EVER MADE WITHOUT
A BOLD GUESS.

Isaac Newton

IN ORDER TO SUCCEED, WE MUST FIRST BELIEVE THAT WE CAN.

Nikos Kazantzakis

GO OUT THERE AND GET IT!

SCARED IS WHAT YOU'RE
FEELING. BRAVE IS WHAT
YOU'RE DOING.

Emma Donoghue

IF YOU WANT TO CONQUER
FEAR, DON'T SIT HOME
AND THINK ABOUT IT. GO
OUT AND GET BUSY.

Dale Carnegie

EITHER I WILL
FIND A WAY, OR
I WILL MAKE ONE.

Philip Sidney

IF YOU BELIEVE
IN YOURSELF
ANYTHING
IS POSSIBLE.

Miley Cyrus

JUST DO YOUR VERY BEST.

IT IS BEST TO ACT
WITH CONFIDENCE,
NO MATTER HOW LITTLE
RIGHT YOU HAVE TO IT.

Lillian Hellman

BE THE CHANGE
THAT YOU WISH TO
SEE IN THE WORLD.

Mahatma Gandhi

COME AT YOUR CHALLENGES WITH FULL FORCE.

LIFE SHRINKS OR EXPANDS IN PROPORTION TO ONE'S COURAGE.

Anaïs Nin

BELIEVE IN YOURSELF.
PICK A PATH THAT
YOU, DEEP DOWN IN
YOUR SOUL, WON'T
BE ASHAMED OF.

Hiromu Arakawa

WE EITHER MAKE
OURSELVES MISERABLE,
OR WE MAKE OURSELVES
STRONG. THE AMOUNT OF
WORK IS THE SAME.

Carlos Castaneda

NEVER DULL
YOUR SHINE FOR
SOMEBODY ELSE.

Tyra Banks

BELIEVE YOU
CAN AND YOU'RE
HALFWAY THERE.

Theodore Roosevelt

THE WORST ENEMY
TO CREATIVITY IS
SELF-DOUBT.

Sylvia Plath

YOU ARE A HERO!

TO WRITE IS TO
INFLUENCE.
TO INFLUENCE
IS TO CHANGE.
TO CHANGE
IS TO LIVE.

Jane Evershed

YOU HAVE TO
BELIEVE IN
YOURSELF
DESPITE THE
EVIDENCE.

Kent Haruf

WE ARE WHAT WE
REPEATEDLY DO.
EXCELLENCE, THEN,
IS NOT AN ACT,
BUT A HABIT.

Aristotle

KEEP SMILING, BECAUSE
LIFE IS A BEAUTIFUL THING
AND THERE'S SO MUCH
TO SMILE ABOUT.

Marilyn Monroe

BE CONFIDENT IN YOUR DECISIONS.

TURN YOUR FACE
TOWARD THE THE
SUN AND THE
SHADOWS WILL FALL
BEHIND YOU.

Maori proverb

IF YOU
DON'T BELIEVE
IN YOURSELF,
WHO WILL?

Ridley Pearson

THE ONLY POWER
THAT EXISTS IS
INSIDE OURSELVES.

Anne Rice

YOU ARE STRONG.

FREEDOM
LIES IN BEING
BOLD.

Robert Frost

NOTHING IS
IMPOSSIBLE, THE
WORD ITSELF SAYS
'I'M POSSIBLE'!

Audrey Hepburn

BELIEVE IN YOURSELF!
HAVE FAITH IN
YOUR ABILITIES!

Norman Vincent Peale

YOU CAN BE SUCCESSFUL.

ACTION IS THE
FOUNDATIONAL
KEY TO ALL
SUCCESS.

Pablo Picasso

WE MAKE THE WORLD WE
LIVE IN AND SHAPE OUR
OWN ENVIRONMENT.

Orison Swett Marden

DO THINGS YOUR WAY.

WHEN YOU HAVE
CONFIDENCE, YOU CAN
HAVE A LOT OF FUN.

Joe Namath

TO BE A GREAT
CHAMPION YOU
MUST BELIEVE YOU
ARE THE BEST.
IF YOU'RE NOT,
PRETEND YOU ARE.

Muhammad Ali

ALWAYS DO
WHAT YOU ARE
AFRAID TO DO.

Ralph Waldo Emerson

WHETHER YOU COME
FROM A COUNCIL ESTATE
OR A COUNTRY ESTATE,
YOUR SUCCESS WILL BE
DETERMINED BY YOUR
OWN CONFIDENCE.

Michelle Obama

NO ONE ELSE HAS YOUR VISION.

PUT YOUR
FUTURE IN
GOOD HANDS –
YOUR OWN.

Anonymous

FOLLOW YOUR
INNER MOONLIGHT;
DON'T HIDE
THE MADNESS.

Allen Ginsberg

DON'T WORRY ABOUT WHAT OTHER PEOPLE THINK.

YOU ARE NEVER TOO OLD
TO SET A NEW GOAL, OR
DREAM A NEW DREAM.

Les Brown

MAGIC IS BELIEVING
IN YOURSELF, IF
YOU CAN DO THAT,
YOU CAN MAKE
ANYTHING HAPPEN.

Johann Wolfgang von Goethe

REMEMBER,
NO MATTER
WHERE YOU GO,
THERE YOU ARE.

Confucius

IF YOU ASK ME WHAT
I CAME INTO THIS LIFE
TO DO, I WILL TELL
YOU: I CAME TO
LIVE OUT LOUD.

Émile Zola

DARE TO DO IT!

WHAT WE DO
FLOWS FROM
WHO WE ARE.

Paul Vitale

YOUR SOUL IS ALL THAT
YOU POSSESS. TAKE IT
IN HAND AND MAKE
SOMETHING OF IT!

Martin H. Fischer

YOU
DON'T
KNOW
WHAT
YOU'RE
CAPABLE
OF UNTIL
YOU TRY.

IT TAKES COURAGE TO
GROW UP AND BECOME
WHO YOU REALLY ARE.

E. E. Cummings

BELIEVE AND
ACT AS IF IT WERE
IMPOSSIBLE TO FAIL.

Charles F. Kettering

IF YOU'RE GOING TO
DOUBT SOMETHING,
DOUBT YOUR LIMITS.

Don Ward

ORDINARY ME CAN
ACHIEVE SOMETHING
EXTRAORDINARY BY
GIVING THAT LITTLE
BIT EXTRA.

Bear Grylls

WE MUST HAVE
PERSEVERANCE
AND ABOVE ALL
CONFIDENCE IN
OURSELVES.

Marie Curie

DARE TO BE
HONEST AND FEAR
NO LABOUR.

Robert Burns

NOTHING IS IMPOSSIBLE.

WITH THE NEW DAY
COMES NEW STRENGTH
AND NEW THOUGHTS.

Eleanor Roosevelt

BIG SHOTS ARE ONLY LITTLE SHOTS WHO KEEP SHOOTING.

Christopher Morley

I CAN,
THEREFORE I AM.

Simone Weil

WHAT THE MIND CAN
CONCEIVE AND BELIEVE,
AND THE HEART DESIRE,
YOU CAN ACHIEVE.

Norman Vincent Peale

THE BEST WAY TO
PREDICT YOUR FUTURE
IS TO CREATE IT.

Abraham Lincoln

BE BRAVE. TAKE
RISKS. NOTHING
CAN SUBSTITUTE
EXPERIENCE.

Paulo Coelho

BE THE MASTER OF YOUR DESTINY.

EVERY ARTIST
WAS FIRST AN
AMATEUR.

Ralph Waldo Emerson

WE ARE ALL OF US
STARS, AND WE
DESERVE TO TWINKLE.

Marilyn Monroe

WHEN I LET GO
OF WHAT I AM,
I BECOME WHAT
I MIGHT BE.

Lao Tzu

THE KEY TO SUCCESS
IN LIFE IS USING THE
GOOD THOUGHTS
OF WISE PEOPLE.

Leo Tolstoy

LIGHT
TOMORROW
WITH TODAY!

Elizabeth Barrett
Browning

SHOW THE WORLD WHAT YOU'RE MADE OF.

TRUST THE DREAMS,
FOR IN THEM IS HIDDEN
THE GATE TO ETERNITY.

Kahlil Gibran

IT IS NOT THE
MOUNTAIN WE
CONQUER BUT
OURSELVES.

Edmund Hillary

YOU GOT THIS.

If you're interested in finding out more about our books, find us on Facebook at **Summersdale Publishers** and follow us on Twitter at **@Summersdale**.

www.summersdale.com